THE KITCHEN SINK PRAYER BOOK

Bernadette McCarver Snyder

LIGUORI
PUBLICATIONS

One Liguori Drive
Liguori, Missouri 63057
(314) 464-2500

Imprimi Potest:
John F. Dowd, C.SS.R.
Provincial, St. Louis Province
Redemptorist Fathers

Imprimatur:
+ Edward J. O'Donnell
Vicar General, Archdiocese of St. Louis

ISBN 0-89243-217-9
Library of Congress Catalog Card Number: 84-80871

Cover design by Pam Hummelsheim

Interior illustrations courtesy of
Sears, Roebuck and Company

Copyright © 1984, Liguori Publications
Printed in U.S.A.

I dedicate this book to today's Christian homemaker — who never has enough time, enough patience, or enough help. Now she will at least have enough prayers!

I wish to thank the family who has put up with THIS home-maker — her traumas and trifles, predicaments and prayers. And I thank God for his loving tolerance and enduring ear.

Bernadette McCarver Snyder

Introduction

What's a "Kitchen Sink Prayer Book"? It's a book with prayers about all the little irritations, aggravations, and exultations that are the ingredients in the recipe for everyday life — prayers about everything including the kitchen sink!

Since family life is sometimes funny, so are the delightful illustrations which were taken from a 1908 Sears Roebuck catalog. They depict simple household items that were in use at a time when the home was truly the center of life, the hub of family activities, and a security blanket as well as a launching pad. Maybe all homes can be that way again someday — if we all pray hard enough.

In other times or other places, other people may have thought that you had to go to a mountaintop or a monastery to pray. That sounds great to me because I am always glad to go ANYWHERE — but the truth is I spend more time by the running water of my sink than by the running water of a mountain stream. So my prayers are often on the run, in between, off the cuff, off the wall, anywhere, anytime. But God is everywhere — so I think prayer should be too! I hope you agree.

WHERE DID THAT expression come from, Lord: ''everything BUT the kitchen sink''? The kitchen sink is the one thing that I have had enough of! I have given it some of the best hours of my life — and it has given me some of the worst!

I have worked in it, near it, and sometimes under it! That sink is where I have doused, diced, sprayed, prayed, and hoorayed.

That's where I have washed plates caked with dried egg yolk and tennis shoes caked with dried mud; washed potatoes, tomatoes, and rutabagas; and washed my mouth out with soap after replying to the question, "How do you like housework?"

But no matter how much I might complain about it, I am grateful, Lord, for my kitchen sink. Decorating experts may tell you that the perfect home must have an epergne as a centerpiece for the dining room, an exotic plant as a cornerpiece for the family room, and an expensive bit of bric-a-brac as a conversation piece in every room — but, Lord, the only thing a home really needs is a kitchen sink and a good kitchen to go with it.

The kitchen sink is sometimes a centerpiece or a cornerpiece but always a conversation piece. The kitchen is the place where everyone gathers for midnight snacks and philosophical discussions, for afternoon snacks and secret-sharing, for hurried breakfasts and good-morning, good-bye kisses, and for pot washing and cozy chats after big holiday dinners. It's even the place everyone gathers at a party — after you have put the fancy food and the fresh flower arrangement and the good silver on the dining room table. You can keep suggesting that everyone move out of the kitchen and go somewhere nicer, but no one ever seems to find anywhere nicer. Be they ever so humble, the kitchen and the kitchen sink seem to be favorite places for making memories.

So thank you, Lord, for giving me a kitchen sink and a family and friends to go with it. But, Lord, someday when I am busy at the sink and certain persons keep coming in, saying things like "Why aren't there any ice cubes in the freezer?" "Why aren't there any clean dishes anywhere?" "Where is my favorite glass?" "Why have all my socks disappeared, and why isn't my yellow shirt clean so I can wear it to the ball game?" don't be surprised at anything I might do. I might just climb up on the kitchen counter and stick my feet into the sink to soak and say, "I'm sorry, but I am not taking any more questions today. I am busy making a memory."

Our 75-Cent Dust Protector.

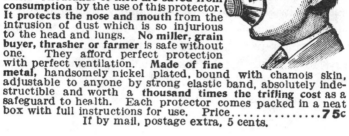

AT LAST! Just what I need, Lord — a dust protector! Maybe I could issue one of those to everybody who comes in my front door, and then I wouldn't have to feel guilty because my house may be contributing to the air pollution problem.

I have tried to pretend that the fine white powder on my furniture is powdered sugar in honor of "Home, Sweet Home." I have suggested that the dust is there so that small children can write their names in it, thereby being encouraged to learn their letters. I have told my furniture, "Dust thou art and to dust thou art — even now — returning."

But, Lord, when children grow up they don't tell their friends, "My mom dusted the house every single day." They remember: "We used to take a bag of doughnuts and go to the zoo real early in the morning when nobody was there — except us and the animals." "We used to go to a farm to buy vegetables, and we would climb the farmer's trees (They were nothing like we had ever seen

9

in our subdivision!) while Mom picked out fresh corn and tomatoes for dinner and laughed with the farmer — and neither of them got mad at us about the trees.'' ''We had the BEST birthday parties and even unbirthday parties!'' ''Home was nice.''

Bless me, Lord, I am not worthy — or perfect. But my house is usually dusted every day — just not always. I am usually on time — just not always. I usually get the laundry separated right so the whites don't turn pink or purple — just not always. And I usually have a place for everything and everything in its place — just not always. Say, Lord, maybe that's what I need instead of a dust protector — a ''usually protector''!

I GOT ALL dressed up to go somewhere today, Lord, but when I looked in the mirror there was something wrong. I tried to figure out what it could be. The new outfit looked OK, and the color was nice. The shoes were the right style, and even the earrings matched. And then I realized what it was, Lord.

It was the face.

That's definitely what was wrong, Lord — the face. There were bags under my eyes, packed full enough to take a trip around the world. And those lines at the sides! I know I am supposed to smile coyly and call them laugh lines. But they are not funny. You and I both know, Lord, that they are wrinkles.

Yes, I hear you, Lord: "Beauty is only skin deep." But that means I'd better do something about that skin! How can I feel good *inside* when I have to keep looking at my *outside* in the mirror every day?

I have become resigned to the fact that I will never be Miss America or Mrs. America or even win the Pillsbury Bake-Off — but, Lord, if you've been trying to make a beautiful "new me" inside, the next time I look in the mirror could you let a little of that come shining through so I won't notice the old me on the outside so much? I know. I know. All this shouldn't matter. But it does, Lord. It does. I have been praying for patience, fortitude, valor, and virtue. Today, Lord, I am praying for a facial, a good haircut, a hot-oil treatment, a mud pack, and a mask to wear until all those spiritual aids take effect.

Kenco Battery Fan Motor.

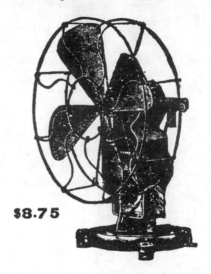

$8.75

WE SIT IN OUR air-conditioned cocoons today, Lord, isolated from your world of nature — no gentle, fanned breezes to waft in the sound of birdsong or children's laughter, no fragrance of honeysuckle on the fence or roses abloom on the bush, no drone of honeybee or chirp of evening cricket. And no neighbor calling to come and chat across the fence to share the day's joys or woes.

Forgive us — forgive me — this comfortable isolation, Lord. Let me see all that I am missing by closing myself in. Help me reach out beyond my comfort zone — to experience again the joy and mystery of your multifaceted, fascinating world. Help me reach out beyond my safety zone to touch your other children who may be in need TODAY of a helping hand or a shoulder to cry on.

Elijah heard you in the gentle breeze, Lord, but all I hear is the whir of my air conditioner. It cools my body — and my reactions. Warm my spirit, Lord. Help me open my ears and my eyes and my heart so I can hear when you whisper. Free me so I can go where your gentle breezes send me.

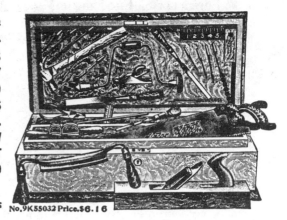

No.9K55032 Price.$6.16

MY HUSBAND has enough tools to tool his way through any household emergency, Lord. A lot of them were given to him at a shower before our wedding — and a lot of them he hasn't used once. But in case he ever needs any tool known to man, it is there on his workbench in the basement.

Why aren't housewives ever given tools, Lord? Oh, I know, we get a lot of blenders and toasters and strawberry pluckers — but never any of the REAL tools we need for our trade, for our lifework. One day we are walking down the aisle in a pretty dress with a bunch of flowers in our hands — and the next day we are expected to know how to turn a house (or an apartment) into a home, with the future of a whole family in our hands.

When I was in school, Lord, I learned a lot about history, math, chemistry, literature, foreign languages, and wonderful other etceteras. These were a great foundation for life, and I am very grateful to have had the opportunity to discover them. But the only thing I remember learning in my Home Economics class was how to make Eggs à la Goldenrod and how to choose a silver pattern.

Do you know how to make Eggs à la Goldenrod, Lord? You fix a cream sauce (not the best way to start a morning), mix in the chopped whites of hard-boiled eggs, pour this over toast, and then push the yellow of the egg through a tea strainer and sprinkle it over the sauce to make it look like little flecks of goldenrod!

Not once have I had an urge to make that at my house in the morning — when I am always running ten minutes late, a horn is blowing because the car pool is early, the cat is meowing because I forgot to give him his catfood à la liver, somebody has just knocked over the box of crunchie-wunchies and somebody else has just stepped in the spill, crunching the wunchies all over the kitchen floor. No, goldenrod eggs was not a tool I needed.

And as for the silver pattern, I couldn't afford the one I chose so I settled for one that was similar and soon learned that that was one of the patterns of family life — not getting what you choose but what you can afford! But that's only a pattern, Lord, not a tool.

Lord, we housewives and mothers need a good tool kit. But none of the stores carry them — so we turn to you. Help us, Lord.

Give us the patience to weather every crisis — so our children will at least THINK we are calm and strong enough to steer our waterlogged canoe through the waves. Give us an understanding ear so we can hear and try to heal every hurt — so our family will never hesitate to turn to us for help. Give us imagination — so we can turn even a meatloaf into a celebration and make family gatherings memories to cherish. Give us a sense of humor — so we can laugh at ourselves and with our family.

And help us to use these tools wisely, Lord, so we can build the kind of home that is nailed together by faith and hope, with little niches chiseled out for quiet times and big rooms added on for the overflow of friends and plenty of open windows to let in the sunshine of laughter and love.

THE POMPEY PUMP.

$1.49 PER PAIR

A NEW SIDE LACE.

$1.64 PER PAIR

I'M SURE GETTING a kick out of today, Lord — and it's all because of you! You made the sun shine through my kitchen window; you sent a redbird to perch in the tree on the patio; you put a giggle in my heart and a skip in my step; and you even made my hair curl for once this morning!

Who but you, Lord, could think of such rainbow ways to cheer our days: the sound of spring raindrops on the rooftop; a flower suddenly bursting into bloom to surprise us as we step out the front door; a sunset with purples and blues slashing through the gold to perk us up as we're driving home after a long, hard day; a smiling baby sitting in a supermarket cart who goos and coos at us as we pass by. All your creations, Lord — all alleluias. Thank you, Lord, for this alleluia day.

Fine Style.

$2.98

I WISH SOMEONE could tie a ribbon 'round me today, Lord — to make me feel fancy, special, out of the ordinary. I'm tired of being ordinary, Lord. I want to be champagne and caviar instead of peanut butter and jelly. I want to have heads turn when I come into a room. I want someone to notice me, listen to me, and be surprised at how extraordinary I am!

Yes, I hear you, Lord. I don't need a blue ribbon or a badge of courage or a beauty queen's crown. I have you, Lord. You know what I am and who I am. You know I am special because you made me that way. But, Lord, do you have to keep it such a secret? Couldn't you just whisper our little secret to someone today — and tell them to pass it on?

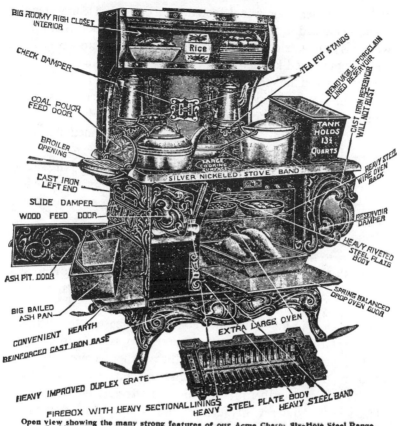

BIG ROOMY HIGH CLOSET INTERIOR

CHECK DAMPER

COAL POUCH FEED DOOR

BROILER OPENING

CAST IRON LEFT END

SLIDE DAMPER

WOOD FEED DOOR

ASH PIT DOOR

BIG BAILED ASH PAN

CONVENIENT HEARTH

REINFORCED CAST IRON BASE

HEAVY IMPROVED DUPLEX GRATE

FIREBOX WITH HEAVY SECTIONAL LININGS

TEA POT STANDS

REMOVABLE PORCELAIN LINED RESERVOIR

CAST IRON RESERVOIR WILL NOT RUST

TANK HOLDS 13½ Quarts

LARGE COOKING SURFACE

SILVER NICKELED STOVE BAND

HEAVY STEEL WIRE OVEN BACK

RESERVOIR DAMPER

HEAVY RIVETED STEEL PLATE BODY

SPRING BALANCED DROP OVEN DOOR

EXTRA LARGE OVEN

HEAVY STEEL PLATE BODY

HEAVY STEEL BAND

Rice

Open view showing the many strong features of our Acme Charm Six-Hole Steel Range. Cooking utensils illustrated are not furnished with range at prices quoted.

HAVE YOU NOTICED, Lord, that we human beings may not always be good at communication — but we are experts at complication? As soon as somebody discovers something, we keep modernizing it until it's almost too complicated to be of any use.

One day somebody rubbed two sticks together and got fire, and, the next thing you knew, somebody had invented a cookstove that had a wood-feed door, a coal-feed door, a damper, a teapot stand, a spring-balanced drop oven door, and an ashpit door. Soon there were gas ranges, electric stoves, toaster ovens, microwave ovens, and computerized kitchens that could be programmed to turn on the coffeepot in the morning, the crockpot at noon, the oven in the afternoon — and have your preprogrammed dinner ready at whatever time you had programmed yourself to come home.

The only problem, Lord, is that every time something is improved, there are just that many more elements that can break. The cave family never had to call a repairman to fix their two fire sticks, but we are always laboring to try to get our laborsaving devices repaired — or to try to make enough money to buy the newest improved models.

Why do we complicate our lives so, Lord? When will we learn to simplify, to stop being possessed by our possessions? Help us, Lord. Show us again the lilies of the field. Show us how to step away from our complicated world long enough to enjoy the simple beauty of your world and your teachings.

But, Lord, in the meantime, could you please help me find a good repairman who can give my oven two aspirins to bring its temperature down . . . and tell my dishwasher we are not beachcombers so it will stop depositing sandy grit on my dishes . . . and tell my refrigerator that it is definitely a refrigerator and not a jet plane so it will quit revving its motor loud enough to drown out the TV . . . oh, and about the TV. . . .

THE TYPE F H HARVARD DISC TALKING MACHINE

$15⁹⁰

DO I SOUND like a broken record to you, Lord? I know I must sound that way to my son. When I listen to myself talking to him I can't believe what I'm saying!

"What's the matter with you . . . can't you hear me?" "Don't talk back to me — and answer me this minute!" "How many times do I have to tell you?"

Of course he can hear me. They could hear me in China. And how can he answer me this minute when I just told him not to talk back to me? But that last one: "How many times do I have to tell you?" is one of the mysteries of the universe, Lord. I will never know the answer to that.

I told him 16,483 times that he should put out the garbage cans on Monday morning and bring them in on Monday afternoon. He doesn't remember me ever mentioning it. I told him ONCE that I liked ONE of his rock records. He never forgot it. Whenever he is breaking the sound barrier with his music and his father frantically shouts a request for him to turn down the noise, my son replies, "But Mom likes it."

I told him 3,986 times that he is nice-looking, intelligent, and fun to have around. He says I never compliment him. I told him once that he was disorganized. He never forgot it. He says he has his own filing system — all that stuff all over the floor is alphabetically thrown — and his mother is always criticizing him.

I have told him a hundred times in a hundred ways what a joy he is as a son. He pretends he has never heard that. But when I "tactfully" suggest that he should wash his favorite jeans at least once a month, he says I am always harping on the same subject and his mother is a born complainer.

You see, Lord? There is no answer to the question, "How many times do I have to tell you?"

Is that the way you feel about me, Lord? You have told me a million times in a million ways how much you love me. And still I sometimes question you. You have told me how I should live — by giving me the commandments and the Beatitudes and your Church and Scripture. And still I sometimes act as though I never heard you.

Forgive me, Lord. Help me to be less of a broken record, repeating my mistakes over and over. Help me to listen and learn and obey and live in such a way that you will know I have heard. But, Lord, WHEN is my son going to learn that his skateboard should not be stored on the sofa and his dirty clothes should not be used as a doorstop? How many times do I have to tell him, Lord, how many?

REDUCED TO $ **4**⁹⁸

LORD, AS YOU KNOW, my husband has always been brash — but now he's gotten brassy! Out of a clear blue afternoon, he suddenly announced that he thought we needed a brass headboard for the bed in the "master's" bedroom.

Until then, he had never shown any indication that he even knew our house had furniture. If I bought any new household item, I had to point it out to him so he wouldn't fall over it. So this sudden pronouncement from the top brass made me come to attention and salute.

I immediately got down to brass tacks, found a great sale on brass headboards, brought one home, and even talked my son into helping me assemble it. When my husband came home and I pointed it out to him, so he wouldn't fall over it, he was surprised and delighted.

There was only one problem, Lord. As soon as I put up that headboard, the rest of the room looked funny. The pictures were in the wrong place; the lamp wasn't right any more; and even the curtains didn't have enough class to go with the brass.

It's going to take me weeks — or maybe months — to find the right lamp, the right curtains, the right placement for the pictures, and get everything reassembled again.

Why is it, Lord, that every time I make a small change in my life for the better it just sets off a chain reaction? If I get a new dress, I have to start searching for shoes to match. If I get a new hairdo, I have to take time to learn how to keep it looking that way — and probably buy a new hair dryer. If I get a new sofa, I have to reupholster the chair that suddenly looks too shabby to stay in the same room with it. If I plant flowers around the patio, I have to find time to weed and water them. It never ends, Lord.

Unfortunately, that doesn't seem to happen in my spiritual life. If I make one small change for the better — decide to say a morning prayer or read Scripture ten minutes a day or talk the family into sharing a short prayer time every night — that seems to be the end of it. I think I'm being so "good." I don't need to do anything else or to grow any further. Fortunately, Lord, YOU don't let me get away with that. You keep pulling me back, putting new challenges and new opportunities in my life and calling my attention to them so I won't fall over them. Thank you, Lord, for setting off so many chain reactions in my life — to intrigue me and inspire me, in spite of me.

OUR $1.85 GOLD FILLED SPECTACLES.

$1.85

BOY, AM I GETTING nearsighted, Lord. I just can't seem to see around corners or into the future. And sometimes I only see the bad things because I'm too close to the problem to be able to see any good in it.

The other day my son and I were supposed to meet my friend and her son for lunch (a rare occasion and therefore notable). We wanted to go to a certain Mexican restaurant because we had some half-price coupons. So we made elaborate plans to rearrange our day and to rendezvous at a certain place at a certain time. We were all on time. We found parking places. We were delighted with ourselves — until we got to the front door of the restaurant. A tiny sign announced that they would be closed for two months for remodeling.

It was time to go to Plan B.

I have a friend who enjoys swimming, and whenever a free day comes along we try to arrange to go to the pool together. Something always happens: a sudden thunder shower; a weird fungus that attacks the pool; a weird virus or cold germ that attacks one of us; a weird motor stoppage that attacks the car.

We go to Plan B.

Sometimes I think Plan A has become the twilight zone or the Bermuda triangle of my life, Lord. No one I know ever seems to get there, and, if they did, I'm sure I would never hear from them again. On the other hand, Plan B has become a way of life.

Does everyone have this problem, Lord? Is it a phenomenon of modern life? Is this the American Plan or the European Plan or your plan? Are you just trying to see if we're paying attention? We are, Lord, we are.

Although Plan B always seems much less desirable to me, I have to admit that it usually turns out to be a lot more fun or a lot more exciting than Plan A could possibly have been. And I don't even have to put on my glasses to see that.

So, forgive me, Lord, for being so nearsighted that I still keep yearning for A when you give me B. But could you just let me try Plan A once, Lord — so I could see how bad it would have been? And then I, of little faith, won't have to make a spectacle of myself yearning anymore.

THE REFRIG-ERATOR has an ice capacity of 100 pounds and is a splendid size for large families. It has beautifully carved northern elm case, in high gloss golden finish. Solid brass hinges and locks, and the best quality galvanized steel linings, galvanized ice rack and provision shelves. It has a removable waste pipe and our improved trap to prevent the entrance of warm air. A swinging front baseboard.

ECONOMY REFRIGERATOR $14.35

ECONOMY LARGE DOUBLE DOOR FAMILY REFRIGERATOR
COLD, DRY AND ROOMY. PERFECT INSULATION, PERFECT CIRCULATION AND PERFECT PRESERVATION OF THE FOOD.

OLD ICEBOXES are back in, Lord, but for a long time they were out — usually out on the back porch. That's when people would say, "If only I had an electric refrigerator instead of an icebox I would be happy."

They also said: "If only I had a car, so I wouldn't have to ride the streetcar, I would be happy." "If only I had TWO cars instead of one, I would be happy." "If only I had a television instead of a radio, I would be happy." And others said, "If only I had a million dollars . . . if only I could become a movie star or big league ballplayer . . . if only. . . . "

I guess the if-only virus is easy to catch, isn't it, Lord? It's been around a long time. Someone probably said, "If only I had a bigger pyramid, I would be happy." or "If only Rome could be built in a day. . . . "

Why is it, Lord, we always think THINGS — or people — will make us happy? "If only I had a husband . . . " "If only I had a baby . . . " "If only my husband would talk to me . . . " "If only my children would obey me. . . . "

Help us, Lord, to stop waiting for someone else to come along and find happiness and give it to us — when all the time it's right inside each of us. Real happiness comes only from you, Lord, but please help me remember that the only one who can make me happy on earth is me. Happiness is mine for the finding, but I have to look for it and work for it and hope for it and pray for it — and recognize it when I come across it!

Forgive me, Lord, for waiting for my husband, my offspring, my friends and relatives to MAKE ME HAPPY — when all the time I'm the only one who can do the job.

But, Lord, if only I could find one of those "economy large double door family" refrigerators that cost only $14.35, I'm sure that would make me happy — at least for a little while!

THIS HAS CERTAINLY been one of those nose-to-the-grindstone days, Lord. After I got breakfast on the table and off again, fixed the sack lunches, drove the car pool, stopped at the cleaner's and the library and finally made it back home, I had to hurry and get the grocery list made, the beds made, the chicken casserole for the church social made, the dentist appointment made, the pie for supper made, the after-school lemonade made, and all the other things made that might be made by a maid if I had a maid — but I don't.

The day is disappearing, and I don't feel like I have made a dent in my chore list — even though I have made a mess of the kitchen, made a wreck of myself, and made some sarcastic remarks about my role in life.

Sorry, Lord, I don't mean to complain. Actually, I like my little grindstone. It couldn't fit my nose any better if I had made it myself. I like my cozy little chores, even if I never seem able to get them all to fit into my cozy little schedule. Thank you, Lord, for giving me the opportunity to do things for my family and friends and church. Even though, some days, it seems like a grindstone existence, I know that my being here has made a difference. And when I look around at all the things I have done, I can be proud to say they were all "homemade."

I'VE GOT TO GET a better handle on my life, Lord!

I've finally become resigned to the fact that I don't have any pull and certainly not enough push. But, Lord, you and I both know that I should at least be able to get a handle on what I do have. Help me, Lord.

Help me clean out my linen closet, my garage, and my mind. Help me pitch out all those hems-and-haws and put in some get-with-its. Help me replace the "what ifs?" with some bright new "why nots?"

Help me see that your love can give me enough push to handle anything. Help me remember that I DO have a friend in high places! You are my friend, Lord. And who needs more pull than that?

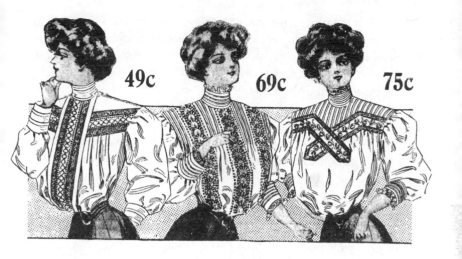

49c **69c** **75c**

I FOUND the cutest blouse this week, Lord. I was so pleased because I had been looking for something to perk up that blue jacket that's nice but boring. I just knew this would be just right for it! It was just wrong.

But as I was packing up the blouse to return it, I remembered that I had an old suit that same color. I got it out, and they looked like they had been made to go together. The new blouse made my old suit look completely different and brand new. It was like getting a whole new outfit for the price of a blouse!

I've noticed that happens in my life a lot, Lord. I bought that lamp, thinking it would be just right next to the sofa — and again, it was just wrong. Then I sat it over in the corner by the rocker — to get it out of the way until I could return it — and it was perfect there, just what we had been needing to brighten up that corner. Do you send me on these detours, Lord, because you know that's the only way I will ever wind up at the proper destination?

I remember when I signed up for that course at church because I thought I needed to meet some new people and make some new friends — and then almost everybody there was someone I already knew. But the discussion leader was so fantastic that I learned a lot of new things about you, Lord, and about Scripture and about prayer and about myself, too. I would have been too lazy to sign up for that course just to LEARN something; but you detoured me there anyway, didn't you, Lord?

Thank you, Lord, for all the little surprises and detours that make life interesting. Thank you for all the discoveries and delights I encounter on the side roads and gravel paths while I am struggling frantically to get back to the highway.

And when I set my sights on a certain goal, absolutely determined that nothing will deter me or change my course, thank you for never saying a discouraging word. Thank you for letting me struggle along, with my teeth gritted and my brow furrowed, while you gently change the course and give me what I need instead of what I want. And when I discover I like where I am much better than where I thought I wanted to be, thank you for not saying "I told you so."

19c

44c

**GENUINE TRUE
BLUE ENAMEL**

I HAVE GROUNDS for divorce, Lord — from my coffeepot. It keeps surprising me by leaving little gritty grounds in my morning cup of coffee. It's not nice to fool mother in the morning, Lord.

It also makes such weird, gasping, gurgling noises that visitors are always looking suspiciously toward the kitchen, wondering if there's a crazed goldfish in there battling its way upstream in my sink full of soapy dishwater or a hyperactive hippopotamus blowing bubbles

Of course, the coffeepot isn't the only appliance that has turned against me. The dishwasher must think this is a bank because it keeps leaving deposits of dried egg yolk and oatmeal on the plates. The no-frost refrigerator keeps frosting up, the hot-water heater keeps shutting down, and the oven does not bake at the temperature I tell it to — so when I expect to get ''somethin' lovin' from the oven,'' I'm in for another surprise! What am I going to do with these appliances, Lord? They are acting just like children — and I never know what to do with them, either!

Forgive me, Lord. I know I should be grateful for all of today's wonderful laborsaving devices, but my devices seem to think that the term "laborsaving" means they don't have to work!

Could you have the appliance angel come down and tell them that it's the lady of the house who's not supposed to have to work? And then could you have the housewife angel come down and tell the lady of the house to quit drinking coffee and finding fault, to call in the repairman or the garbage man to either overhaul or haul away her troublemakers, and then to start looking at her own faults for a change?

Like the goldfish or hippopotamus, I'm always swimming upstream or blowing off steam. Slow me down, Lord, and show me how to float in the pond where you have planted me. Help me to start perking again, to stop frosting up or overheating. And show me that prayer is the best laborsaving device — because when I ask you for help first, Lord, the job is always easier.

MY LIFE IS a list, Lord — a list of groceries to buy, errands to run, phone calls to make, dinners to plan, bills to pay, faults to correct, goals to achieve, dreams to dream, and rainbows to follow. I eventually manage to cross off most of the chores on the list, but the faults are still there — and where am I going to find time for the dreams and rainbows?

Lord, woman does not live by chores alone. Don't let the chore list make me so listless, Lord, that I will forget the faults and goals and lose sight of the dreams and rainbows. Only you, Lord, know the real me — the one without a grocery sack or dishcloth in her hand. Help me to find her again and show her how to daydream and stargaze and pray and exult again — without having to make a list.

LET A SMILE be my umbrella? It isn't raining rain, it's raining violets? Lord, yesterday I tried letting a smile be my umbrella; and if I hadn't gotten those wet clothes off the minute I got home and jumped into a hot shower, I would have had pneumonia. That was not a bouquet of violets that soaked me to the skin, made my gutters overflow and the basement leak, Lord.

Did you forget to turn off the tap? Do you realize you have generously let it rain on our parade and our neighborhood for SIX days now, Lord? Surely, on the seventh, you will let us rest!

A little gray goes a long way, Lord. Do you know what it's like to look out the window in the morning and see the gray dawn, gray sky, gray rain, gray air, and gray prospect of it getting any better? We need a little blue and gold in our weather, Lord. Of course, maybe I shouldn't say "we." Rain may look drab and depressing to me, but my son loves it. He says it is mysterious, exciting, and a chance to pretend he's a secret agent in London. He lets mystery be his umbrella.

I know that's the right attitude, Lord: to make the best of it, to remember that we need rain for the crops and the flowers and the grass. No, better not think about the grass and how fast it'll grow after all this. Better not think about all the muddy footprints I'm going to have to mop up this afternoon. Better not think at all — that shouldn't be too hard! Better just lie down and read a good book or take a nap and forget about it. Say, maybe there IS something good about all these rainy days after all. Thanks for my dry, snug house, Lord, and forgive me for being such a drip.

MIRROR, MIRROR on the wall, shame on you! Don't you know I am getting sick of seeing sags and bags, wrinkles and crinkles, and that extra twenty pounds that I have let go to waist? Couldn't you look the other way sometimes and tell me I am ALMOST the fairest one of all?

Lord, Lord, what am I doing talking to the mirror — when I should be spending my time with you? Remind me, Lord, that we should all be mirrors of you — reflecting your teachings and your love. Imperfect, still struggling, yet showing forth enough of your glory so that anyone we meet will see a small reflection of what it means to be a Christian.

Help me remember, Lord, that you can only be seen in the world through your followers — so I better keep my reflection polished up a little better!

But Lord, would it be all right if I go out shopping today for one of those antique mirrors — you know, the kind that is dark and shadowy because the glaze has become crazed? Then, maybe, when I peek into the mirror in the morning and only a shadow-glazed figure gazes back, I won't be so crazed by what I see!

IF I COULD ONLY nail down some of the loose boards of my life, Lord, things sure would be simpler. If I could only stop walking around feeling guilty all the time, with this prickly irritation at the back of my head, nagging me that I've forgotten something.

I always feel like I've left a loose board flapping in the wind somewhere in my day or in my life — something unfinished that should be finished, something undone that should be done, somebody neglected that shouldn't have been.

I don't mean to forget, Lord; it's just that I have to go in so many directions all at once. There's always something that I should be remembering to do for my husband, for my offspring, for the house, for the office, for a committee at church — and even for myself. I try, Lord, but I just can't seem to nail fast enough.

I'm tired of always being in a flap, Lord. Soothe me. Guide me. Show me how to nail down my priorities so that instead of just coping with the wonderful life you've given me I can learn to enjoy it and exult in it.

I LOOK AROUND my kitchen this morning and — beyond the pots and pans — I see miracles everywhere, Lord. I see food kept cold and fresh in the refrigerator, bacon cooking almost instantly in the modern magic of the microwave, muffins baking in the gas oven, coffee perking in the electric percolator, and dishes being washed in the electric dishwasher.

But these are just the kind of miracles the world has learned to make, Lord. I thank you for the more important ones. I thank you for my eyes that can look out the kitchen window and revel in the beauty of the flowers blooming on the patio, my ears that can hear the children laughing, my nose that can smell the fresh coffee brewing, my tongue that can taste the fresh-baked muffins and cold butter, and my mind that can savor and treasure all the happenings of this day. Thank you, Lord, for the miracles of my every day.

Don't ever let me be so busy or so foolish that I will forget to see and appreciate and glory in the heavenly kind of miracles that only you can create.

**Famous Non-Pa-Rell House-
hold Rubber Gloves.**

86c

I ALWAYS SEEM to have my hands in water, Lord — washing dishes; rinsing out stockings; watering the indoor plants, the outdoor plants, the lawn, the bushes, and the cat.

Actually, I have to water the cat twice. I put water in his cute little cat bowl, and he daintily sips from it while I watch — but then I have to remember to put water in a second place to handle the bad drinking habit he indulges in when he thinks I'm NOT watching. He has developed a secret cat craving for plant water!

He discovered that one of my indoor plants is a swimmer — with its roots firmly planted in water instead of dirt. I don't know how his peculiar drinking habit got started, but this cat likes that plant water so much he must think it's cat champagne. But — he feels guilty when he drinks it.

He waits until he thinks I'm busy. Then he eases himself across the room, trying to keep a low profile, and quietly starts to lap up the illegal libation. If he glances up and sees me watching him, he looks away in embarrassment and slinks low as a caterpillar into the kitchen.

I guess we all do that, don't we, Lord? We find something we like to do, but we think it might not be quite right — not REAL bad but maybe not quite right. So we wait until we think you're not watching, and then we indulge. We always feel guilty and embarrassed about it because we KNOW you saw us.

Forgive us our catnips, Lord. And keep us out of hot water. Help us to grow up and be mature enough not to do anything that would be embarrassing if we got caught doing it. But, Lord, please don't tell anyone that I ate that whole candy bar today and, then, put whipped cream all over my low-cal dessert.

THE MISSISSIPPI CLOTHES WRINGER,  $3¹⁶

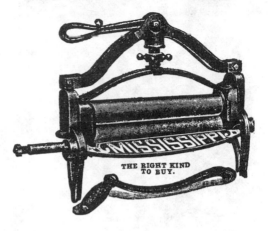

THE RIGHT KIND
TO BUY.

I'VE BEEN BAD today, Lord. All morning I've been making a list of the people I'd like to put through the wringer! I've been thinking up smart remarks that I SHOULD have used when certain people made insulting digs or sarcastic comments about me or mine. I've fervidly found fault, taken long looks at everybody else's shortcomings, and fondly focused on others' flaws and foolishness. I've been callous, critical, cutting, and cruel — and I've enjoyed every minute of it!

Sorry, Lord. I know I shouldn't be thinking those thoughts, even in the privacy of my little yellow kitchen. I should be thinking happy thoughts, UP thoughts, hopeful thoughts, with peace and good will toward all. But even a quiet little teapot has to let off steam sometime, Lord, and today was my day. I've gotten rid of so much venom and rottenness this morning that my whole body should start glowing with health and good cheer any moment now.

So, forgive me, Lord. And thank you for letting me get all wrung out where nobody else could hear — or answer back.

KENWOOD BALL BEARING BACK GEARED STEEL WINDMILLS

$13.75

WINDMILLS ARE FUN but frustrating, Lord. They look so pretty, whirling and swirling in the breeze, but they never get anywhere! They're always hurrying and scurrying, gone with the wind but forever staying put just where they were planted. Does this remind you of me, Lord?

My life is fun but frustrating too, Lord. I enjoy the whirling and swirling, hurrying and scurrying — until I start worrying about the fact that I never seem to get anywhere. And then I remember, Lord. I don't really need to get anywhere — except to heaven.

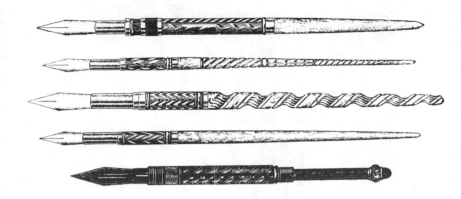

I USED TO THINK I had to have my pen in hand at all times, Lord — just in case you decided it was time for a test. And if I scored high, you would love me; but if I failed, you would turn away and I would be alone, working to win back your friendship. I know now that you love me even when I fail.

I know you want me to do well, to score high, and not have to go to the corner and hang my head; but I know, too, that even if I falter you will go on loving me and helping me to do better next time.

And, Lord, I guess the homework of life is a little like the math homework I had in grammar school. Sometimes there would be pages of "problems" to work out — problems that were similar but different — and I had to work on them, over and over. But, after all that practice, I would finally get the knack of doing it. And then they weren't really "problems" anymore because I knew how to get the answers.

Thank you, Lord, for giving me the tools of prayer and faith to work on my problems. And since I seem to get so much practice, maybe someday I'll even get the knack of solving them.

$1.23

98¢

WHEN I WAS a little girl, Lord, do you remember how every Sunday morning my mother would see to it that I was dressed in my best, with a big bow in my hair, and off we would go to church? Do you remember when the collection basket was passed my father always handed me some money so I could be the one to drop in our family's contribution? Sometimes I was tempted to put at least a little of the money in my pocket, Lord, but I didn't. And I felt very proud and grown-up.

After I was married and going to church with my own family on Sunday morning, I noticed my husband always gave our son the donation to drop in the basket. And I noticed other fathers did the same. It occurred to me that that's the way you give your gifts too, isn't it, Lord? You give the gift to your children and then wait for them to pass it on.

Thank you, Lord, for the gifts you have given me. Help me to be generous and pass them on to others — even though it is sometimes hard and I am often tempted to hug them to myself. Thank you for entrusting me with such gifts as imagination, joy, hope, and the gift of gab. Help me to spread them around — to enrich your other children and to give honor to their Father.

I'M BORED WITH my ironing board, Lord. I want to donate it to a toothpick factory or use it to build a nice fire in the fireplace.

I'm tired of crimping collars and cuffs, steaming seams, and hemming and hawing over hems that won't straighten up and iron right.

I thought perma-press would solve all my pressing problems, but there are still all of those little unexpected crumples and rumples and crinkles and new wrinkles — in my life as well as in my ironing.

Help me learn to cope, Lord — to see a crumple as a challenge and each new wrinkle as an opportunity to iron out my troubles. But don't be too mad at me, Lord, if someday you notice that ironing board leaving home — riding in the back of a garbage truck.

I'VE BEEN GOING crackers, Lord — but no more! I'm here today to ask you to help me stop being in the soup all the time.

I'm tired of crumbling the minute somebody touches me, of cracking in two at the first word of criticism or advice. I'm tired of salting my day with tears of frustration and irritation. It's time to grow up — to toughen up.

Lord, help me learn to accept constructive criticism but be confident enough in my own self to recognize my good qualities too. Help me be mature enough to try to change my faults without dwelling on my shortcomings. Help me see myself as imperfect without being crushed by it and wilting into despair. And help me learn to laugh at myself sometimes, Lord — to not take everything so seriously. Help me see the positive instead of always the negative. Empty me of all that self-recrimination, Lord, so there will be room for your love and joy. Teach me to face the day and the criticisms with a smile.

Show me, Lord, that instead of going crackers, it's better to simply say "cheese"!

ISN'T PERFUME wonderful, Lord? It all looks pretty much the same except for the packaging, and it's all probably made of about the same ingredients. And yet . . . one perfume can remind you of a young girl's nosegay; another scent conjures up a picture of a mysterious femme fatale; and still another makes you think of moonlight and roses.

Perfume Atomizers.

No. 8K3043

No. 8K3044

Our price.....29c
Unmailable.

I remember when my son was about six years old and my mother often came from out of town to visit us. She always wore a marvelous perfume that was expensive and extraordinary. Her clothes, her hair, even her purse had that special fragrance. Since the two of them would spend a lot of time sitting very close, reading books and sharing secrets, one day I asked my son how he liked Grandma's perfume. He said, ''Perfume? I just thought ALL old people smelled like that.''

Like the perfume, Lord, we're all made of the same ingredients and look pretty much the same except for the packaging; and we, too, convey different images — of innocence or worldliness, romance or mystery or whatever. But wouldn't it be nice, Lord, if, as we grow in age and wisdom, we could emit a happy fragrance?

Maybe it would be the fragrance of patience, the essence of experience, the aroma of time spent listening to small children and making them believe that we really care what they are saying, the scent of a life well spent.

Show us, Lord, how to live so that we will age well. Help us see each day as a potpourri of opportunities, a time to make the kind of memories that we will be able to enjoy and savor in years to come. Teach us to yearn not so much for the sweet smell of success as for the aroma of holiness.

$35.35

PEARL
VALVE
BUTTONS.

IT TAKES A LOT of hot air to blow your own horn, Lord —
but that's just what I've been doing. Sorry about that.

I know I am puffed-up, vain, and not as important as I try to
make myself sound — or try to make myself believe. I know I am
nothing without you, Lord, but I need you to remind me sometimes. I need you to help me tone down the horn-tooting and hot air
and to turn myself down a few decibels before somebody else
does.

Help me learn to blow YOUR horn, Lord, instead of mine. Help
me trumpet your truth and make your love my clarion call. Without
you, Lord, I am but a clanging cymbal — and the people around
me are getting pretty tired of my orchestrating my whole life with
clangs and clashes. But WITH you, Lord, I could make beautiful
music, find the lost chord, and finish Schubert's Unfinished
Symphony. Oops . . . there goes the horn again. Sorry about that,
Lord.

PLOWING AND PLANTING — that seems to be my whole life, Lord. Every day I keep trying to plow through my son's room, thinking there must be a kid in there somewhere! And I am always trying to plant seeds of caution, of good manners, of clean living, of religious fervor.

The plowing has gotten me nowhere. I can get a furrow made through the piles of smelly socks, school projects, empty root beer bottles, telescopes, microscopes, and dissected frogs — but the next day the path has disappeared and it's time to start plowing again. No matter how hard I try, I have never been able to get that field cleared of debris.

And as I am planting, Lord, I keep thinking, "The kingdom of heaven is like a man who sowed good seed in his field. While the people were sleeping, his enemy came and sowed weeds amidst the harvest and then went away."

Lord, we try to sow good seeds in our families, and then the enemy comes and sows weeds through TV, movies, rock music lyrics, peer pressure, and even some school programs. Show us what is happening while we are sleeping, Lord. Help us be alert enough to notice when the weeds start growing — and show us a way to weed out the bad influences before it is too late.

The plowing we will have always with us — and I have gotten used to furrowing through the ant farms and the overdue library books and the backpacks still packed with dirty clothes from last week's hike and the footballs, baseballs, and dust balls. But, Lord, I need your help in the planting.

Help me — help us all, Lord — to weed and seed carefully enough so we can cultivate in our children a respect for your teachings and lead them to your rich harvest of love.

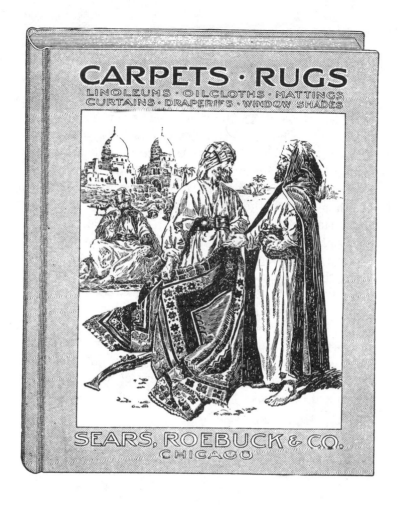

I NEED A magic carpet, Lord; but I don't think Sears carries them anymore. I've got to find something to "take me away from all this" for a while — just a little while. I'm so tired, always so tired. I need a refreshing flight of fancy. I need to soar above it all so I can look back at my daily routine and see what I would be missing without it.

Why is it, Lord, that housewifing seems to make you tireder than any other occupation? I never feel rested anymore, and my friends tell me they have the same problem. I guess it's because we have a job that's never finished. Other workers have a certain task assigned for the day; and, even though it may be hard work, they finish it and go home. The housewife never finishes.

As soon as the house is straightened and the kitchen cleaned after breakfast, it's time for lunch. As soon as the floor is mopped and dry, little feet — and big ones — start dirtying it again. And as soon as the kids finally get new outfits, they start outgrowing them. A housewife's whole life can be spent trying to finish jobs — just to start them again.

But, Lord, I guess you know how it feels. Your world has the same problem. As soon as the frilly, young green leaves are on the trees and the bushes are blossoming and golden daffodils are waving on a hill and spring is in full spring, it's time to start on summer. And as soon as the sun is shining bright enough to get everybody out of the house to look at summer in full bloom, the leaves start falling and it's time to get to work on autumn.

Thank you, Lord, for the magic carpet of our ever-changing but never-changing world. Help me to remember how beautiful the pattern is and how lucky I am to be a part of it.

$1.39 $1.85 $1.25 $1.48

WHERE HAVE ALL the children gone, Lord? It doesn't seem too long ago when children were supposed to be "seen but not heard." They never had to think up clever answers so they could "dialogue" with the adults. All they had to do was skip rope, play hopscotch, and curl up in the front porch swing — watching bees hum around the honeysuckle and dreaming the kind of dreams that only children can dream.

Today so many children are expected to act like short adults. They are expected to take on responsibility, get involved, stay busy, and take care of themselves — and sometimes take care of the house too. Any free moments are spent in front of the TV instead of playing. And they learn so much of the world so soon. No more time for hopscotch and honeysuckle.

Maybe it's good for them. Maybe being adult all their lives will make them better grown-ups. I hope so. But I miss the innocent, carefree, childlike children, Lord. Don't you?

Sure Waker Alarm Clock with Switch.

No. 20K6175 This is an Alarm Clock which, when placed in the circuit of an ordinary bell outfit, using a switch in place of a push button, will wake the soundest sleeper. Price of clock with switch $1.15
If by mail, postage extra, 24c.

THANK YOU, LORD, for the person who invented the alarm clock. Without it, I might have slept through my whole life. But now I need a different kind of alarm clock, Lord, one that will keep me alert during the day!

A basement that has sprung a leak, making my downstairs look like a lakeside resort . . . a lawn that's turning into a dandelion-decorated jungle . . . a pile of laundry that is growing so fast I will soon need mountain-climbing equipment to scale it — all will eventually get my attention. But I need to be alert in a different way, Lord.

I should notice when someone needs an understanding ear or some kind of help NOW — instead of at three o'clock when I will be through mopping the floor. I should notice when someone needs to be told that life is worth living and things will get better. I should be there to say, ''You are attractive, intelligent, competent, fun to have around, IMPORTANT to me — and to others,'' before it is too late to break the pattern of self-doubt and low self-esteem.

Help me, Lord, to hear when family or friends sound the alarm. Even if it is only a subtle rustling in the air, let me hear, Lord — as you always hear me.

MOVING PICTURES

A FIVE-CENT THEATER with moving pictures? Gee whiz! Golly Ned! Holy cats! Were those the good old days?

Today's days seem awfully good to me, Lord, but I do sometimes wish we could return to simpler times. When I was growing up, movies cost a lot more than five cents; but we went every week and sometimes twice a week. That was the most wonderful form of escapism, a way to forget all our troubles and go home feeling refreshed and often inspired.

You forgot everything as you sat in the darkened theater, munching popcorn and watching the big screen. You discovered how other countries looked, how other people lived and thought and dreamed. You experienced adventure, romance, suspense. And the movie either had a happy ending or a sad but inspiring one where someone gave his or her all for a cause or a country or a love.

Today it's nice and convenient to have television in our homes, Lord, but it just isn't the same. Even when they put *Gone with the*

Wind on TV, it was hard to get excited watching the burning of Atlanta on a little seventeen-inch screen in the corner of our bright and busy family room. There were as many moving pictures in the room as on the screen — somebody moving to the kitchen for a snack, somebody moving to answer the telephone, somebody moving to put out the cat — and at every crucial moment a commercial. No, Lord, it just isn't the same.

Of course, we seldom see a happy or inspiring ending anymore. No one sacrifices or endures hardship for others. No one lives happily ever after. The children's shows are full of violence, and most of the others are either blatantly or subtly immoral.

They say this is the real world and that escapism is immature and unrealistic. But, Lord, if you escape your world for a while, when you come back to it you can see it from a different perspective. Even when you go on vacation and have a wonderful time, it's good to come home. You appreciate its welcoming comfort, no matter how humble it is. If we never get away, how can we appreciate coming home?

And if our children never see the hope of a happy ending or an inspiring story of self-sacrifice, how can they ever aspire to something higher or want to serve mankind or even live happily ever after? Well, Lord, if the movies aren't going to do it, I guess it's another job for Super Parents. We're going to have to give our kids what the movies don't. Help us, Lord. Help us to inspire them to aspire and show them the possibility of happy endings — especially the happy ending of coming home to you.

BEFORE NOON TODAY, Lord, I am supposed to come up with a cute idea for an invitation to the ladies' luncheon, an exciting idea for a class field trip, a clever idea for my husband's birthday party, and a never-been-done-before idea for a club program. So far, the only idea I have come up with is the idea that I would love to find a nice comfortable hammock and take a nap.

I cannot tell you, Lord, how much I want to take a nap. All I can think of is the gentle swinging and swaying of a hammock slung between two tropical trees — preferably in Hawaii. And there I am, soaking up the sun, becoming beautifully bronzed, dreaming lazy daydreams, listening to the splash of some distant waves, and sipping a tall, cool iced tea.

I'm tired of being an ''idea person'' — the one everyone runs to when they need something ''clever'' for any occasion from a kindergarten coronation to a leapfrog festival. My idea bag is empty; my clever has gone dull; and my dream machine wants to take a nap.

Don't get me wrong, Lord. I'm grateful that you gave me the silly, offbeat kind of mind that thinks off-synch, is stuffed with "such stuff as dreams are made on," and takes flights of fancy and fantasy. It's fun thinking funny!

But it's tiring, too. So, Lord, don't tell anybody — but I am going to take the phone off the hook and pretend the back bedroom is Hawaii and treat myself to a nice, long nap. Maybe while I'm napping, I'll have enough daymares to help me dream up all the ideas I need today.

To get in the mood, maybe I'll sprinkle some of that tropical orchid perfume on my pillow and leave the shower running so I can pretend it's a tropical waterfall. Say . . . maybe the birthday party could be a Hawaiian luau, and the ladies' luncheon could have a Midsummer Night's Dream theme, and the class field trip could . . . .

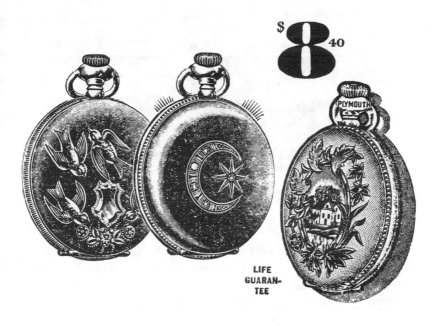

$8 40

LIFE GUARAN-TEE

PLYMOUTH

I THINK I NEED a pocket watch, Lord. Then maybe I could save a pocketful of time for myself each day.

My wristwatch couldn't help me manage that. I never have time on my hands. It always runs right through my fingers!

My alarm clock isn't the answer. Even if I set it a half hour early so I'll have more time, I sleep right through it.

And as for the clock in my car — that will never save me any time. It's just like the clock in everybody else's car — it has never worked!

So, Lord, could you please ask Santa to bring me a pocket watch next Christmas? And, in the meantime, help me get my personal time machine ticking better so I can save a little time each day for myself — and for you.

Genuine Ever Ready Flash Light.

SHOULD BE
IN EVERY
HOME.

98ᶜ

MOMMIES ARE SUPPOSED to be like flashlights, Lord —
ever ready. Ready to pass out first aid, lemonade, Band-Aids, and
always financial aid.

Well, my battery's running low, Lord. My first aid is second
class; my lemonade has turned sour; my Band-Aids have been in
the cabinet too long and have lost their stick-em-up; my financial
aid can no longer be banked on — and I'm the one who's about to
pass out!

Fill me with your light, Lord, so I can get my glow back. Help
me to shine on with the harvest moon, be brighter than Rudolph's
red nose, glisten like spring rain on the sidewalk, and gleam like a
summer sunbeam. Of course, if I do all that, Lord, people will
stare at me suspiciously — wondering if I am smiling happily
because I know something they don't know or if I just don't
understand the situation.

Maybe I DO know something they don't know, Lord. I know
you are with me all days, loving me in spite of my failings, picking
me up when I fall down, and putting your own special Band-Aids
on my bruised ego and hurt feelings. That should be enough to
make me glow, even in the dark! And then I WILL be like a
flashlight!

SOUND THE ALARM, Lord. Where there's smoke, there is not always fire! Today I was slaving over my hot stove as usual — browning some meat — and suddenly, a piercing, ear-shattering wail filled the kitchen with clamor and filled me with instant panic. For a few seconds, I thought there must be a banshee in the bamboo bookcase or a hyena in the hydrangea.

Finally, I realized it was the smoke alarm. The burnt offering I was cooking for supper had triggered it — and it certainly got my attention. I suddenly realized that that's what I am sometimes, Lord — smoke but no fire. I fume and fuss, complaining and griping and finding fault and sending out loud wails that signal panic when there should be none. I waste my energy, sending up smoke signals when there's no fire.

And, Lord, sometimes I put up a smoke screen between myself and those I love — clouding the issue with my own petty hurts and problems, hiding behind my own self-interest, refusing to let them in, refusing to fight my way through the smoldering misunderstandings to see their side of the story.

Help me, Lord, to be more than smoke and fury. Help me to catch the fire of your love and spark it in others. And thank you, Lord, for the smoke alarm to warn me, for the meat for my supper, and for your understanding ear to listen to all my banshee wails.

I'VE GOT TO CLEAN out my cabinets, Lord. Every time I open the pantry door, something falls out. Having a rolling pin roll off the shelf onto your head or being beaned by a can of beans is not a dignified way to start a day.

I've got to learn to organize, systematize, coordinate, formulate, classify, and simplify. In other words, I've got to throw out a lot of that junk.

Help me, Lord, to do the same with all the wrong ideas that have given me an overstuffed head. Help me to pitch out the gossip, the criticism, the faultfinding, the self-seeking, the negative, the trivial. Help me clear the brain, Lord, so that when I open the mouth I won't be embarrassed by what falls out.

9c FAMILY SIZE, HOLT'S OR CYCLONE
IMPROVED EGG OR CREAM BEATER.
Just ask your dealer his lowest
price.

THE FLARE DOES IT.

I'M ALL MIXED UP today, Lord. I'm hurt. I'm mad. I'm sorry for myself. I think my family is all scrambled up and a bunch of bad eggs who have gone off for the day, leaving me at home feeling beaten down, stirred up, and whipped.

I want to run away from home and become an airline stewardess or sit down and eat a pound of chocolate candy. But I've already eaten too many pounds of something, so I can't become a stewardess; and I can't run away because my car is sleeping — even when I kicked its tires I couldn't get a start out of it. And that makes me even madder.

What's wrong with me, Lord? I know things aren't that bad. My husband will call any minute now and say he's sorry. He always does. And my son isn't even aware he hurt my feelings.

He lives in another dimension: tuned in to his rock music, busy with his computer and his schoolwork and his plans to colonize another planet since his old planet (like his old mother) is on the way out. He will come wandering in this afternoon, happy as a clam and just as talkative, expecting me to have cherry pie and milk and a smile waiting to greet him. If I am teary-eyed and pouty, he will be shocked because he won't be able to imagine ANYTHING that could have happened to upset me.

Why do I always overreact, Lord? And when I am disturbed, why do I always blame somebody else? Why do I start listing all the things that are wrong with my husband, find fault with my offspring, criticize the world at large? Why do I always look "out there" for the cause of the problem, the reason for the hurt? Why do I wait till last to look "inside here" — at me, myself, and I?

Why is it so easy to give all the guilt away and never save any for myself? When I'm cutting the cherry pie, I will probably manage to save at least a small piece for myself, but I'm much more generous when I'm dishing out the blame.

Forgive me, Lord. If I'm mad at my world, part of it is definitely my own fault. Help me to realize how I sometimes irritate others and trigger the upset. Help me to see my own faults first and others' last. Help me to grow up and get a thicker skin.

And besides, if there are bad eggs at my house, it is probably because I have spoiled them rotten. So, I'd better get busy and whip them into shape. But first, Lord, I think I'll just spoil myself and leave the housework for awhile and take a nice walk. Maybe I'll walk down by the shopping center and look in the windows or go in the gift shop or the dress shop or get a cup of coffee. Maybe I'll even buy a pound of chocolate candy!

I HAVE A TERRIBLE confession to make, Lord. It's a deep, dark secret that I can discuss only with you. If I told anyone else, I would be stared at, sneered at, and laughed at. Only you could understand, Lord. The terrible truth is — I want a tricycle.

I know some company makes adult-sized tricycles because I've seen them advertised. It seems they're used in retirement communities where residents feel they are no longer quite agile enough to ride a bicycle. The truth is, Lord, I never WAS agile enough. I could never balance enough to get that second foot off the ground. Yes, I know, I've always been a bit off-balance anyway.

All these years, I've seen people whizzing along, hair blowing in the breeze, faces ruddy from being whipped by the cool wind, looking carefree and agile on their two-wheelers — while I trudged along, two-footing it.

But I figured even I should be able to manage a nice, sturdy, steady three-wheeler. I saved the ad I saw, trying to build up my courage and my bank account enough to order one. Then, this morning, a friend called and said she had the funniest story to tell me. She said one of her ''older'' neighbors had actually bought an adult tricycle to go grocery shopping and was happily wheeling around the neighborhood on errands until she went around a corner too fast, lost her balance — and fell off her tricycle!

I don't know if I could handle that, Lord — explaining a scraped knee, sprained ankle, or black eye by saying I fell off my tricycle. Maybe I'm still not mature enough to be well-wheeled.

I guess I am destined to stay a foot soldier in the army of life. So thank you, Lord, for giving me two sturdy feet that can take me down the primrose paths and through the forest trails. Maybe if I was whizzing along with my hair blowing in the breeze, I would miss the violets growing in the shadowy side paths and fail to notice the bird's nest on the highest branch or the white fluff of a tail on the baby bunny hopping away through the brambles.

But, Lord, I noticed the kindergartner who lives next door has been flying around the neighborhood on this little contraption made of plastic that has two huge big wheels and a seat that is slung so low that it can't be much more than three or four inches off the ground. There is no way he could fall off it because it looks like he's almost sitting on the ground as he whizzes past with the wind blowing in his face. Do you think they make THOSE in an adult size?

THE NEW 1908 MODEL MOTIOGRAPH

WE DON'T HAVE a Motiograph at our house, Lord, but we do have a box that projects moving pictures into our family room — along with moving ideas, values, and temptations. I'm beginning to think that today's television is so moving, it should be moved right out of our house!

From the moment our children are born, Lord, we are busy trying to "program" them. We program them to walk, talk, eat with a spoon, read, write, and say their prayers. We try to program them with the values and morals you gave us in the Ten Commandments, Lord. But today they are being programmed by something that is often more powerful than their parents. They look to television for guidance instead of to us. This machine now dictates styles, habits, and manners as well as the social and moral attitudes that are considered the ''norm'' for our current society.

When are we going to wise up, Lord? When are we going to get smart enough and brave enough to complain about this kind of programming? If we invited a guest into our home and the guest continually taught our children that immoral, violent behavior was the ''norm'' — acceptable and desirable — we would quickly invite the guest to leave. But only a few of my friends have been courageous enough to tell the television to get out.

When I was growing up, Lord, we were taught about the ''occasion'' of sin. We were told that it was best not to even allow ourselves to be put in a situation that would be a temptation, that could lead to or ''occasion'' sin. And now almost every family in our country has an occasion of sin right in their home.

Help us, Lord. Help us to get mad with righteous anger — mad enough to fight back. Mad enough to write the television stations, the sponsors, the producers, and even the stars — to complain about the smut and to demand better programs. Television is such a wonderful invention — it can entertain and delight and inspire and could improve the quality of our life instead of degrading it. It could be an occasion of joy instead of an occasion of sin — if only we would demand it. Help us, Lord, to be demanding — to prove that care and prayer can be even more powerful programming than soap operas!

Neat Embroidered Bonnet.

23¢

Poke Bonnets

42¢

AS LONG AS THERE ARE baby bonnets, Lord, isn't there hope for us all? Those tiny, frilly bits of fluff are made to cover and protect a precious head still small enough to be filled with only innocence and purity.

Forgive the loss of innocence in our world, Lord. Help us save our children. Help us save ourselves. Give us the faith and courage to speak out against the pollution of smut. Help us recover the joy and peace of childlike trust and simple goodness.

MY CANDLE BURNS at both ends, Lord — and that makes it hard to find a candlestick!

I love the flame of excitement in today's fast-paced life-style. I delight in the bright light of all the possibilities, all the sights to see, all the doors to open. I bask in the warmth of the opportunity to have a home, a family, a career, hobbies, continuing education, travel, and fun, too.

But I still have only a 24-hour day, Lord. I know I can't be all things to all people. I can't even be all things to myself. My candle has been burning too brightly for me to be able to get a hold on it. Help me, Lord. Light my way. Show me which parts of my life I should keep burning brightly and which ones I should snuff out.

Help me to center my dreams and goals and shining hopes on you, Lord, and never lose sight of your burning love that is the beacon to guide me, the warmth to cheer me, and the flame to light up my life.

THE KING OF WRINGERS.

Guaranteed for five years.

$**4**.71

A DOUBLE TUB. That's what I'm becoming, Lord — a double tub. I went shopping for a new outfit today, found one I liked, and blithely took it into the fitting room and tried it on. That's when the fat hit the fire, the cookie crumbled, and I could see that I had been taking the cake! Lord, what I saw in that mirror was a sight for sore eyes. It made my eyes so sore I cried all the way home.

I have evidently been chewing the fat with my friends and neighbors once too often — or twice or thrice or twenty times too often! But there's no use crying over spilt milk. It is obvious that it is time for me to stop living off the fat of the land, start talking turkey, eat crow — and go on a diet!

From now on, the only kind of pie I will eat is humble pie. And I am going to bite the hand that feeds me — every time it starts to reach for something fattening. This time, I am going to cut the mustard and really do it . . . no, not do it — diet. And if I don't lose at least ten pounds in the next two weeks, I will eat my hat. (It will probably taste delicious by then!)

Help me, Lord, to stick to my guns and forget the gums. Show me that a taste for life is better than a taste for pizza. Help me learn to bite my tongue — and nothing else. Help me think of a balanced diet as a piece of parsley stuck in each cheek.

I know I can do it, Lord, because I have come across some wonderful diets. There's the Little Miss Muffet diet — where you eat only a few curds of cottage cheese and a small glass of wheyfully delicious skim milk. There's the Little Jack Horner diet where you suck your thumb at mealtimes instead of eating. There's the Old Mother Hubbard diet where you keep your cupboard bare so neither you nor your dog will be tempted to snack.

With imaginative diets like that, I know I can get rid of those ugly pounds and stop looking like Humpty-Dumpty. Instead, I am going to look slim as a willow and thin as a reed. (That's probably what I should be eating — willows and reeds.) But, Lord, in case — just in case — I bite off more than I can chew and the diet doesn't work overnight and I have to eat my words, help me to swallow my pride and keep trying. Words and pride are two of the few things that have no calories, so it will be safe to keep eating and swallowing them. Then, with your help, Lord, I know I can do it . . . and diet.

I'M GOING AROUND in circles today, Lord. And I think whoever invented the wheel shouldn't have — because today's wheeled vehicles just keep us in a spin.

I just took my four-wheeled automobile back to the repair shop for the FOURTH time. Why couldn't they fix it right the first time, or why did it have to break in the first place? I know, I know; cars don't break, but you know what I mean. When the wheels don't roll right or the gears gum up or the carburetor chokes or whatever, it's broken.

And then the other wheeled vehicle we own — my son's bike — got a flat tire. After spending all morning in the auto repair shop, I had to spend all afternoon trying to get the bike into my probably temporarily repaired car to get it to the bike repair shop to have a *new* tire put on because the old tire had been repaired so much it couldn't be repaired anymore. I know, I know . . . that's a ridiculous sentence that would not make a dandy diagram, but you know what I mean.

When we got home, we decided to put together the rolling slack rack that I just bought. It came unassembled — of course — and had 5,126 pieces in little plastic bags. I know, I know . . . that's an exaggeration, but you know what I mean. After reading and rereading the misleading directions, assembling and disassembling and much disgusted discussion, we finally got the rolling rack put together. But did it roll? Of course not.

Where will it all end, Lord? We buy something guaranteed to last a lifetime — and it lasts till the next Tuesday. We pay extra to get the better quality model, and it breaks down before we can get it home. We are constantly repairing and replacing, buying, throwing out, and starting over. We are tired.

And what makes it even more painful, Lord, is that sometimes we buy something really cheap because we are broke, and we decide to just ''make do'' with the cheapie for now and then buy something better when it wears out. It NEVER wears out!

Well, Lord, maybe all these unexpected emergency repairs and all the coping and groping are good for the soul. Maybe it will make us strong and persevering and force us to have true grit. I sure hope so; but, so far, all it has done is make me weak and perspiring and force me to grit my teeth.

Lord, it looks like I've been going around in the wrong circles and spinning my wheels. So, circle me with your contentment and peace today, and help us get all our wheeled inventions back on the right track.

69¢

SOME DAYS IT'S EASY to think that life is a grind, Lord, but it's a lot more fun to think of it as a find!

Every day you put all these little bits and pieces in our life for us to discover — people and places, songs and phrases, new ideas and old ideas with a new twist. We can choose to use them or lose them.

Life can seem like a grind if you're in a hurry and get in the only line at the supermarket that isn't moving — but it can be fun if you use that time to do some "people watching." (People say — and do — the funniest things!)

Life can seem like a grind if you are the "designated driver" in the family and spend so much time in the car you are planning to redecorate it with a philodendron planted in the ashtray, a Dairy Queen poster of a hot fudge sundae on the ceiling, and a smoke alarm on the brake pedal. But it can be an adventure if you sometimes vary your appointed rounds by trying a shortcut that takes you down a charming little street you've never seen before, if you stop for a cup of tea or take a minute to browse in an interesting looking curio shop, or if you really observe the people and places on the corner every time you wait for a red light to change.

Life can be dutiful and still be beautiful. So thank you, Lord, for our daily grind. Help us to make it into a daily double of discovery and delight.

LORD, WHY DID you make men and women so different — and then expect them to live together happily ever after?

Yesterday I brought home this lovely handmade pillow. The design was a colorful bouquet of flowers, and each flower had been carefully stuffed with a bit of perfumed cotton. This gave the pattern an eye-catching 3-D effect, and the subtle perfume filled the room with a gentle fragrance. I loved it. All day I kept passing by the sofa where I had carefully placed it, admiring my new purchase and enjoying the sweet aroma. I wondered if my husband would notice it when he came home.

He did. When he sat down to read the newspaper, he got this funny look on his face and his nose started twitching. Finally, he said, "I think you'd better check out this room — there may be something dead in here. I detect a strong odor of formaldehyde."

This is the same man who said my special four-hour recipe for Beef Bourguignon wasn't quite as good as my "other recipe for stew"! He never notices when I am wearing a new outfit but sometimes says, "Is that new?" when I am wearing a three-year-old dress. Why, Lord, why?

We never see things from the same angle, hear the same messages, feel the same feelings, or think the same thoughts. But if we did, Lord, I would have gone through life and missed all those things he sees and hears and feels and thinks — and then shares with me. Thank you, Lord, for forcing me to widen my horizons in this special way. But help me remember this the next time I show him the darling new earrings I just bought and he smiles and says, "They look like little Brussels sprouts."

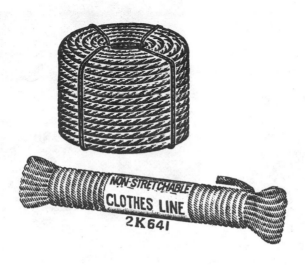

WHY DO I KEEP getting all tied up, Lord?

I promise myself that I absolutely will not volunteer for any more committees, church projects, or field trip "adventures." Then, the next thing I know, I am scheduled for meetings Tuesday and Thursday mornings, church activities for half the weekend, and have been chosen to volunteer to go on a caterpillar hunt or a peanut butter cookout or a leapfrog marathon with the grade-schoolers or chaperone a rock music survival contest at the high school.

Could you please teach me how to say "no," Lord? It should be fairly easy to put two letters together — first the "n" and then the "o." What's so hard about that? Why do I have so much trouble with that word, Lord?

Maybe it's your fault. Do you WANT me to be tied up? Is that where I belong at this point in my life? If it is, help me to be wise, Lord, to know when to say "no" to the things that don't matter so I will have enough time to say "yes" to the things that do. And help me, Lord, to unwind enough to enjoy it, so I won't always feel that I'm at the end of my rope.

WELL, LORD, HERE I AM on the shelf, just like a can of tomatoes — waiting for somebody to come along and discover me and sweep me off the shelf and make me into something delicious. When am I going to get enough get-up-and-go to get up and go and make something of myself MYSELF?

In my pantry, Lord, the only way you can tell a can from a can't is by the ingredients listed on the label. So I just looked at my own ingredient listing and, unfortunately, this is what I found: ''I can't . . . '' ''I don't know how . . . '' ''I'm afraid to try . . . '' ''What will people think . . . . ''

How can I get rid of all those ''additives,'' Lord? How can I get back to the natural ingredients you put into me when you made me — faith, hope, and gumption?

I saw a sign the other day, Lord: ''Success comes in cans, failures in can'ts.'' Help me remember that, Lord. If I'm like a can of tomatoes, then all I have to do to achieve success is to get my can off the shelf!

13^{85}

No. 26K23I

THE THREADS OF MY LIFE start breaking, Lord, every time I even get near a sewing machine. I cannot sew a fine seam. I cannot even manage a sew-sew seam. I get on pins and needles every time I think about "a stitch in time saves nine." That means if I hem and haw and put off that seamy sewing job until tomorrow, I will have nine times as many stitches to take as I would have to take today — and I can't even thread my way through today's!

Why is it that somebody else can whip up an elegant evening gown, a three-piece suit, and a baby's beruffled, beribboned christening dress while I am still trying to figure out how to sew up a rip in my son's shorts before he outgrows them?

Of course, I know several people who are artists with the needle and thread; but they could never make mushroom chicken or French-chocolate mint sticks like mine, so I guess it all evens out. You planned it that way, didn't you, Lord?

Some can sew or paint or sing or tell good stories or play a concerto. Some can be nuclear physicists or mathematicians or professors or helicopter pilots. And some can make a house a home.

If you had given us all the same gifts, Lord, life would be pretty lopsided — and peculiar. If everybody could sew but nobody could cook . . . if there were lots of mechanics but no farmers . . . if the world was full of musicians but no doctors — we'd be in a lot of trouble.

And besides, if everybody had the same gift, nobody could ever give anybody else a gift! Nobody could ever do something for you that you couldn't do for yourself. Nobody could amaze you with their talent or delight you with their ingenuity or surprise you by fixing something you thought was unfixable.

So thank you, Lord, for passing out so many splendid and special gifts — and for spreading them around in such a wonderful way. Thank you for giving each of us our own unique gifts and talents so we can share with others. And thank you, most of all, Lord, for the gift of your love.

$8.15

HOORAY FOR TODAY, LORD! The snows have melted and there's a touch of spring in the air. To celebrate, I went out in the backyard to swing and sway a bit in the glider my teenage son and I put together last summer. And I was in for a sad surprise.

When we bought that glider I had no idea it was going to come in 346 separate parts — metal supports, nuts, bolts, and a LOT of wooden slats. Each slat had to be sanded and shellacked and dried (my job) and then attached, one at a time, to the frame (my son's job). We thought we would never get it finished; but, when we did, it was a wonder to behold — the honeyed sheen of the shellacked slats contrasting with the glistening black metal frame. We were so proud.

All summer we enjoyed the soothing, relaxing sway of the swing as we rested in the shade — and congratulated ourselves on a job well done. And then autumn came. The glider was too large and heavy to move inside, so I resolved that I would find a large piece of plastic to cover and protect it during the winter. But before I got around to it, the icy rains began and then the snows. I looked out the windows — through the snow — and the slats still looked honeyed and safe, so I thought it didn't matter.

It did. Today when I went to sit on the glider, I could see all the bare spots where the shellac had worn off, leaving the golden slats looking like they had gray measles. And it was all my fault. Evidently, I didn't shellac the swing carefully enough in the first place. And then, when I still might have been able to save it by covering up my mistakes, I never got around to it.

Is that the way I handle the rest of my life, Lord? Am I in too much of a hurry to do things right the first time? Do I do a slapdash job in my relationship with my family and friends — when I should be working harder and being more careful? Do I neglect to protect the beautiful blessings that are right in my own backyard?

Forgive me, Lord. Thank you for all the wonderful honeyed moments you've given me. Help me to cherish and protect what is mine to have and to hold. Remind me never to be measly with my time or my love — so I can protect myself from waking up some spring morning with the gray measles!

MY COLANDER AND I are holey, Lord, but not holy.

My unholy but holey colander has a good reason to have strained relationships — with spaghetti, beans, lettuce, and the lot. But I have strained relationships too, Lord, and I don't have a good reason — or even a good explanation. All my excuses have holes in them!

Forgive me, Lord. Help me to handle the strain in this hurry-up-and-wait world. I want to be strong and patient and kind and true-blue. I want to be whole instead of holey. And I want to be holy, too.

Fill my empty spots, Lord. Speak to me through the Scripture. Show me how to follow the example of your apostles and saints. Help me to trust completely in you so that I won't think of my everyday problems as strains. Help me to see that I CAN be strong. I CAN be patient. I CAN be whole. I can even be holy if I truly and totally believe that you are my friend and you will show me the way. But, Lord, please don't let it strain our relationship if I don't become wholly holy overnight. It may take a while.

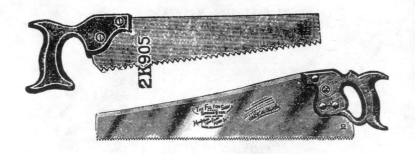

I'M FULL OF OLD SAWS today, Lord. "It is better to give than to receive." "It is better to have loved and lost than never to have loved at all." "Let a smile be your umbrella on a rainy afternoon." "Put your best foot forward." "Bloom where you are planted." I'm full of old saws — and I am sick of them!

Lord, I am tired of always giving and never receiving. Today I want somebody to think about me, to surprise me, to please me, to let me know what it feels like to be on the receiving end for once. I want to love and win instead of lose. I want to stop smiling through all those rainy afternoons and have a happy, sunny afternoon. I want to stop putting my best foot forward just to have it kicked out from under me. And I am tired of blooming in this greasy kitchen where you have planted me. I want to be transplanted to a Hollywood movie set or a New York nightclub or a Paris fashion salon or just a nice restaurant that has tablecloths and doesn't serve hamburgers.

Yes, Lord, I know. I am a pot that wasn't watched, so I boiled over. I am a squeaky wheel, hoping to get the most oil. I put all my eggs in one basket and got cracked. But I feel much better, Lord, now that I have let off some steam, blown my cool, and let it all hang out. Just knowing that you are there to listen and understand calms me and refreshes me and helps me laugh at my silly little frustrations. Thanks, Lord, I needed that — because, for me, a grouch in time saves nine.

A WASHING MACHINE that even a child can run! Lord, I wonder what advertising genius first came up with that idea: "Simple enough for a child to put together; easy enough for a child to operate." It sounds great, doesn't it? But what about something simple enough for an adult?

I remember the time I dragged home an antique sewing machine and had the great idea that, if I could get the top off and the motor out, it would look smashing with a fern planted inside the frame. I worked an entire morning trying to dismantle that machine. And then I had another great idea. I called my six-year-old and his playmates to come in from the backyard and "help" Mommy. Within a half hour the top was off; the motor was out; the kids were back in the backyard, building a jet plane around the displaced machine motor; and I was humming happily, planting my fern.

Of course, every housewife knows that any child can take apart anything in your house within minutes — so why shouldn't a child be able to put something together? That's what children do all day anyway: make things with building blocks, assemble those little snap-together plastic pieces into strange, imaginative arrangements, and use the shovels and buckets in their sandbox to shape, mold, and design everything from castles to space stations. Yes, a child probably could put together some of those things on which I have spent hours, tears, and broken fingernails.

And "simple enough for a child to run" might work too. If you can get children interested in something (that's the hard part!), they can spend hours totally engrossed in even a boring project — like maybe running a washing machine!

They talk about a child's short attention span. Lord, it's the housewife with the short attention span. She puts the wash in, but she can't become engrossed in it because she has a million other things to do while the laundry is washing — wash the dishes, wash the lettuce, wash the windows, wash up some stockings, wash down the spot on the kitchen wall, and try to find time for an afternoon outing so the day won't be a total washout.

Children don't have a schedule; or if they do, they aren't aware of it because Mommy is handling that too. They can concentrate on the job at hand without being distracted by worrying about all the other things they need to do NEXT. They can spend time observing a blade of grass or an anthill or a caterpillar or the sky or the moon or a smile or a mood or a good example or a bad example — things that a busy adult sometimes fails to notice.

Lord, help us to be like children — with attention spans long enough to observe the world around us, to see the things that need changing and the things that need saving, with time to spend building castles and daydreams and memories with the building blocks of imagination and curiosity and sheer joy. And thank you, Lord, for "a little child to lead us."

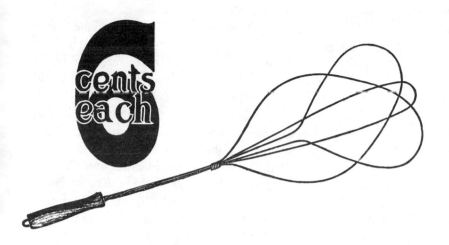

WHEN WE MOVED from a house with lots of shining hardwood floors to this one crammed with carpeting, I sure could have used a carpet beater, Lord. But I would have been tempted to use it on the lady we bought the house from instead of on the carpeting!

That lady loved color! If you stood at one spot in the hall, you could see into three rooms — and what you saw was a bright yellow carpet, a bright red carpet, a bright blue carpet, and the hall carpet which was maroon. We had inherited a rainbow of rugs — and it would have cost a pot of gold to replace them!

I knew I would have to learn to live with wall-to-wall color. And actually, after we got all the furniture moved in and added a few touches, everything looked terrific. We had the brightest house in town; and hardly anybody ever stood at that spot in the hall, trying to view the clashing of the colors.

There was still one problem though — the fiendish family room carpet. It was a heavy shag made of strands of red, tan, and orange. In a certain light, it looked orange, so you couldn't use red accents; but in another light, it looked red, so you couldn't use anything orange. In fact, you couldn't use ANYTHING in that room except wood and sunglasses.

Luckily, I had a lot of old wooden garage sale "junque" to go with a "neutral" sofa and overstuffed chairs and a rocker and lots of green plants and pictures; and by the time we stuffed all that in the room, we beat that carpet into submission. The room turned into one we loved — and lived in.

And there was another bonus, too! I had thought I would miss the hardwood floors from the other house, but all I miss is the hours I spent trying to keep them shined! I can vacuum these crazy carpets in a tenth of the time. And they are indestructible. You can walk all over them without hurting their feelings. You can scuff them and be rough with them, sit on them, spill on them, and insult them like we did when we first met — but with just a little care they bounce right back, bright and cheery as ever.

Just think, Lord, I could have lived my whole life in rooms full of early dull, satisfied to always shift into safe neutral, afraid to fly my colors. Instead, I was forced to discover the fun of these funny magic carpets!

Help me remember the lesson of the Challenge of the Carpets, Lord, every time I come across the unexpected or unfamiliar and decide it is a cloud on my horizon before I give it a chance to be a rainbow.

$ 9.75

I AM A TECHNICOLOR PERSON in a black and white world today, Lord! I feel like I am caught in a time frame for one of those photographs they made with a folding camera, using black and white film.

As I look out my window, everything seems so still and quiet, it feels like time has stopped ticking. The sky is all black and white with a few gray clouds thrown in. And even the clouds look like they're waiting. They're not going anywhere — just hanging around. The drab overcast is like a pall that has fallen on everything, including me. It's as though we're all waiting for the flash of powder to go off and the picture-taking to be finished so we can return to life again — metamorphosing from black and white to living color.

We're waiting for the grass to be green again and the roses pink. We're waiting for the sky to turn blue and for the redbirds to start splashing in the birdbath and for the lilacs to swish their purple fragrance in the afternoon breeze. We're waiting for the technicolor of sunshine and laughter.

Isn't it strange, Lord, how we have to have a gloomy day before we miss the sunshine? We take all your technicolors for granted until they turn gray. Forgive us our nearsightedness, Lord.

Thank you for the gray days that help us appreciate the infinite beauty of the bright ones. Help us learn to take advantage of the stillness of the black and white times, so we can refresh and renew and step back and look at ourselves.

Teach us the art of adding color and sunshine to the lives of others. Then help us to look honestly at our own family portrait and see where we need to do some retouching and brightening. And remind us to say "Thank you, Lord," for the technicolor extravaganza and the brass-band brightness of all the blessings you have splashed upon us. Your camera may have black and white film some days, Lord, but most of the time your rainbow runneth over! Color us grateful.

$44⁹⁵

REMEMBER MY FIRST CAR, LORD? It was about ten years old when I bought it, and it slept late on cold mornings and had a nice big hole in the floorboard so you could watch the world go by as you rolled along the highway of life. But it was my ticket to freedom.

It took me places I couldn't go before. It gave me excitement, suspense, adventure — and gave my mother gray hairs. Driving it made me feel mature and independent — just like the car was! And it was a good and loyal friend — sometimes.

I thought about that car the other day, Lord, when I was in a hurry to get somewhere and suddenly found myself in a line of traffic that was moving at the pace of an inchworm. I thought if I had never learned to drive that first car in the first place, I could have been at home sipping a glass of iced tea on my patio instead of spending the afternoon with a lot of exhaust fumes and exhausting bad temper.

I wished I had taken a different street that day. I wished I could give up my errand and go home. But there was nowhere to turn around. That happens to me every once in a while, doesn't it, Lord? I turn down a road — get involved in a project, make a decision to change my life-style for better or for worse — and then I wish I hadn't; but it's too late to do anything about it because there's no way to turn around.

Thank you, Lord, for giving me the road signs that should keep that from happening too often. Help me to watch where I'm going and to be careful which roads I choose, so I won't end up revving my motor and getting nowhere.

$9^{\underline{10}}$ PAINTS THIS HOUSE

MY HOUSE COULD USE a good coat of paint, Lord — and so could I. We're both beginning to look a little bedraggled around the edges. We may not be as young as we used to be, but I like to think that we have become cozy and comfortable. Maybe that's making excuses or maybe it's facing facts. I'm never sure.

But I am sure that I am very grateful to have a home, a haven. Thank you, Lord, for this blessing, this security blanket. My home may be bedraggled, disorganized, and need a coat of paint, but it looks beautiful to me.

I know if I took all the family pictures off the wall it would be easier to paint. If I got rid of all the plants on the marble-topped table in the family room, I could save the time it takes to water and prune them. If I got modern chrome-trimmed furniture, instead of the wooden antiques and curiosities that I have collected, I wouldn't have to polish carefully with lemon oil. And if I lived alone, there wouldn't be so much cleaning and cooking and somebody always calling me to handle an emergency. I know that "home ties" like these keep me tied up, tied down, and at the end of my rope most of the time — but I hope I am never set free.

Today, Lord, I came across Saint Matthew's passage, "Foxes have holes and the birds of the air have nests, but the Son of Man has nowhere to lay his head." That seems very lonely and sad, Lord, and yet I know that leaves you free to make all our homes your own.

Help me, Lord, to make our home truly Christian and always welcoming, so that you will not come just to visit here but to stay. Come, Lord Jesus. Lay your head in our home. Abide with us. Be our friend. Be our Savior. Keep us in the shadow of your arm — and then nobody will notice that our paint is peeling, our porch is sagging, and the neighbor's dog ate our welcome mat.

WAIT A MINUTE. It will only take a second. Could you hold the phone for a moment? What is this thing called time, Lord?

We're always talking about it as though it is something real. Then yesterday becomes today and soon today will be tomorrow and time flies, time drags, and time marches on.

I heard someone say, "Of course I know what time is — unless you ask me to explain it. And then I know I don't know."

Time is an invention of man — or woman or humankind. (It could just be a plot to make me feel bad since I am so often late.) But our time is not your time, Lord. What seems like forever to us — and could well be forever, our whole lifetime — is just an instant to you. When we pray for something, sometimes it seems like it takes forever for you to answer; but maybe to you it seems like you answered in an instant. So forgive us, Lord, if — when we finally receive what we consider a long-overdue answer to a prayer — instead of saying thanks, we say "Well, it's about time!"

TODAY I'M GOING TO pack up my troubles in this old kit bag and smile, smile, smile.

The art of housewifery may be fraught with frustration — caught in a time capsule with dust, rust, and wear and tear — and bought with toil, tears, and travail. But, Lord, it's still the best job in the world!

Where else could you work on "flex time" — taking time out for hugs and hoorays, stopping for a coffee break or a giggle-and-coo break with the baby, a watch-the-ant-on-the-blade-of-grass break with the preschooler, a shared-cookies-and-confidences break with the fourth grader, or a philosophical solve-the-world's-problems break with the teenager?

Where else could you have a position with the executive power to help shape and mold the values and hopes and dreams of a small person who may hold the future of the world in his or her hands?

Where else could a job description include: spend bright sunny mornings at the zoo, discovering the funny faces and wondrous ways of the animal world; spend lazy afternoons talking over and looking over the mysterious marvels of clouds and caterpillars, rocks and robins, tiny flower petals and mighty oaks; spend evenings with hot chocolate, bedtime stories, and little clean-for-a-change faces smiling up at you as you tuck in the blankets?

Where else, Lord, could you find fringe benefits that include a husband to share love and laughs, a house to turn into a home by using creativity instead of cash, continual challenges and never-ending opportunities to "better yourself"?

Lord, you have packed my bag with so many blessings. Help me — and all housewives — to remember to take them out occasionally, to dust them off lovingly, and to say "thank you."

A house is made of walls and beams . . .
A home is made of love and dreams.

Keep the home fires burning.

Home is the nest you leave, ready for life . . .
And the haven where you can come back to roost.

Home is where the heart is.

It takes a heap of livin' to make a house a home.

A man travels the world over in search of what he needs
and returns home to find it.

There's no place like home.

Home, sweet home.